The Anxiety Blueprint: Tools to Empower

By: Dr. K. Marlowe

ISBN: 978-1-7376283-8-5

Dedication:

To David,

Your friendship and support have always been a source of inspiration. This book is for you, in appreciation of the countless ways you've shown resilience and dedication in your life. Thank you for being a true friend and an excmplary engineer in the light of my chaos creations.

Table of Contents

Introduction: Breaking the Ice

If you find yourself holding this book, it's likely that you've encountered the ever-present companion known as anxiety. Those sleepless nights, the relentless racing thoughts, and the unexplainable fear clutching at your heart – that's anxiety. But fear not, because within these pages, we're about to embark on a journey to a place of peace.

I've witnessed anxiety's powerful sway over countless lives. This book is my attempt to offer you more than just clinical insights; it's an invitation to a shared exploration of understanding and healing.

Together, we will navigate the nuanced layers of anxiety, acknowledging its impact on your well-being. This isn't your typical self-help guide; instead, it's a roadmap crafted with care and rooted in therapeutic principles. My goal is to provide you with practical tools, genuine empathy, and a sense of companionship on your journey.

As we turn the pages, we'll delve into the intricacies of anxiety – its roots, its manifestations, and, most importantly, the strategies to reclaim a sense of calm and control. This is a collaborative expedition, a

space where your experiences and emotions are acknowledged and validated.

So, let's begin this journey together. Whether you're seeking solace, understanding, or actionable steps for change, know that you're not alone. Within these chapters, I aim to illuminate the path toward a healthier relationship with anxiety. Are you ready to take the first step?

Chapter 1: Unmasking Anxiety

Unmasking Anxiety

Anxiety is a multifaceted experience that often wears many disguises, making it difficult to recognize. In this chapter, we'll peel back layers, clarify common misconceptions, and explore the diverse spectrum of anxiety.

You may see anxiety described as the body's natural response to stress. It's a dynamic interplay of psychological, physiological, and environmental factors that can manifest in a multitude of ways.

At its core, anxiety involves interaction between the brain, body, and environment. From a neurological standpoint, anxiety arises from intricate pathways involving neurotransmitters like serotonin and norepinephrine, which regulate mood and stress response. Furthermore, genetic predispositions and life experiences can shape an individual's susceptibility to anxiety, highlighting its complex nature.

Anxiety is not a static condition but rather a dynamic spectrum that varies in intensity and presentation. While some individuals may experience occasional bouts of nervousness or apprehension, others grapple with chronic and overwhelming anxiety that significantly impairs their daily functioning. This diversity underscores the importance of recognizing anxiety as more than a passing emotion but rather an experience.

Anxiety may mask as various other challenges, making it difficult to identify and address. It may manifest as physical symptoms such as tension headaches, gastrointestinal disturbances, or muscle tension, leading individuals to seek medical attention for what they perceive as purely physical ailments. Additionally, anxiety can masquerade as irritability, restlessness, or difficulty concentrating, further complicating its recognition and diagnosis.

By gaining a deeper understanding of the nature of anxiety, we can better equip ourselves to recognize its various manifestations and provide more effective support and intervention.

The Disguises of Anxiety: Recognizing Its Many Forms

The physical symptoms found with anxiety contribute to its deceptive nature. Muscle tension, another hallmark of anxiety, can manifest as tightness or soreness in various muscle groups, particularly the neck, shoulders, and jaw. Tension headaches are characterized by a gripping sensation around the head. Individuals may also experience gastrointestinal disturbances such as nausea, stomach cramps, or changes in bowel habits, which can mimic symptoms of gastrointestinal disorders.

These physical manifestations of anxiety often lead individuals to seek medical attention for what they perceive as purely physical ailments. However, without recognizing the underlying anxiety, these symptoms may persist despite medical interventions targeting their physical manifestations. A challenge may arise if the medical provider decides the patient has anxiety and poorly responds with medical gaslighting. This is not something to expect from a provider but to be aware of if you have anxiety.

In addition to physical symptoms, anxiety can also masquerade as changes in behavior and emotions, further complicating diagnosis. For example, anxiety may present as irritability, causing individuals to become easily frustrated or agitated over minor issues. Restlessness, characterized by an inability to sit still or relax, may also be a sign of underlying anxiety. Difficulty concentrating is another common symptom, as individuals find themselves preoccupied with anxious thoughts and unable to focus on tasks at hand.

These behavioral and emotional changes are not mood swings or personality quirks; they are subtle indicators of underlying anxiety that often go unrecognized and unaddressed. Cultural and societal factors can further obscure anxiety's true nature, making it challenging for individuals to seek help and for healthcare professionals to provide appropriate support.

Demystifying Anxiety: Clarifying Common Misconceptions

To understand anxiety, it's essential to debunk some of the prevalent myths and misconceptions surrounding it. One of the most common misconceptions is that anxiety is simply a matter of overthinking or being overly sensitive. However, anxiety is much more than fleeting worries or nerves before a big event.

Anxiety is a legitimate and sometimes debilitating mental health condition that can affect individuals of all ages and backgrounds. It's not merely a passing phase or a sign of weakness; rather, it's a complex interplay of biological, psychological, and environmental factors.

The Anxiety Spectrum: Exploring Different Levels and Forms of Anxiety

Anxiety is not a one-size-fits-all experience. It exists along a broad spectrum, ranging from mild to severe, and manifests in various forms. Some individuals may experience generalized anxiety, characterized by persistent and excessive worry about everyday events. Others may face specific phobias that trigger intense fear and avoidance behaviors.

Some individuals can experience generalized anxiety disorder (GAD), characterized by persistent and excessive worry about everyday events. For example, a person with GAD may constantly worry about their health, finances, or relationships, even when there is no apparent reason for concern. This pervasive worry can interfere with daily functioning, making it difficult for the individual to concentrate on tasks, maintain relationships, or engage in enjoyable activities.

Others may face specific phobias, which are irrational and intense fears of specific objects, situations, or activities. For instance, someone with a phobia of flying may experience overwhelming anxiety and panic at the mere thought of boarding an airplane. This fear can be so intense that the individual goes to great lengths to avoid flying altogether, leading to significant disruptions in their personal or professional life.

It's important to recognize these specific manifestations of anxiety to provide appropriate support and intervention for individuals struggling with these conditions. It may be easier to consider anxiety on a spectrum to manage the idea of severity when experiencing anxiety.

Additionally, anxiety can manifest as panic attacks, sudden and overwhelming surges of fear accompanied by physical symptoms like rapid heartbeat, sweating, and shortness of breath. These episodes can be terrifying and often lead to a heightened fear of future attacks.

There are anxiety disorders such as social anxiety disorder, obsessive-compulsive disorder (OCD), and post-traumatic stress disorder (PTSD), each with its own set of symptoms and challenges falling at various points on the spectrum.

This understanding is crucial in developing effective strategies for managing and overcoming anxiety in its various forms.

Chapter 2: The Science Behind Panic

Panic attacks involve a complex interplay of biological, psychological, and environmental factors. In understanding anxiety disorders, it's crucial to differentiate between two commonly intertwined experiences: anxiety and panic. While they share similarities, they also exhibit distinct characteristics.

Anxiety typically involves a persistent sense of worry, apprehension, and unease about future events or situations, often accompanied by physical symptoms such as muscle tension, restlessness, and difficulty concentrating.

Panic is characterized by sudden and intense episodes of fear or discomfort, often peaking within minutes, and accompanied by physical sensations such as a rapid heartbeat, sweating, and shortness of breath.

Understanding the distinction between anxiety and panic is essential for navigating the complexities of anxiety disorders. While anxiety may be a constant companion, panic attacks are episodic and intense, often requiring specialized interventions. By elucidating the science behind panic, knowledge and tools can help you better understand and address these challenging aspects of anxiety.

Neurobiology of Anxiety: Simplifying the science behind panic attacks.

Panic attacks are complex neurobiological events involving intricate interactions within the brain's circuits and chemical messengers called neurotransmitters. At the core of panic attacks is the activation of the body's stress response system, known as the "fight-or-flight" response, which is evolutionarily designed to prepare us to deal with threats.

When triggered, the brain's amygdala, a region responsible for processing emotions, perceives a threat and sends distress signals to the hypothalamus, triggering the release of stress hormones like adrenaline and cortisol. These hormones prepare the body for action by increasing heart rate, dilating airways, and redirecting blood flow to muscles.

The locus coeruleus, a small region in the brainstem, releases norepinephrine, a neurotransmitter involved in arousal and stress responses. This surge in norepinephrine contributes to the physiological symptoms experienced during a panic attack, such as rapid heartbeat, sweating, and trembling.

The neurotransmitter serotonin, which regulates mood and anxiety, also plays a significant role in panic attacks. Research suggests that alterations in serotonin levels or sensitivity may contribute to the onset and severity of panic attacks.

The prefrontal cortex, responsible for rational decision-making and impulse control, may become dysregulated during panic attacks, leading to impaired judgment and heightened emotional responses.

Together, these neurobiological mechanisms create a cascade of physiological and psychological responses characteristic of panic attacks. By understanding the underlying neurobiology of anxiety and panic, researchers and clinicians can develop more targeted interventions and treatments to alleviate symptoms and improve quality of life for individuals struggling with these conditions.

Fight or Flight: Discussing the body's stress response.

The "fight or flight" response is a fundamental aspect of the body's adaptive stress response system, designed to prepare us to deal with perceived threats or dangers. It is orchestrated by a complex interplay of neurological, hormonal, and physiological mechanisms, all aimed at enhancing our ability to survive in challenging situations.

At the heart of the "fight or flight" response is the activation of the sympathetic nervous system, a branch of the autonomic nervous system responsible for regulating involuntary bodily functions. When confronted with a perceived threat, such as a predator or a stressful situation, the brain's amygdala, a key region involved in processing emotions and detecting threats, triggers a rapid sequence of events.

The amygdala sends distress signals to the hypothalamus, a region of the brain responsible for regulating hormone release and the autonomic nervous system. In response, the hypothalamus activates the body's stress response by signaling the adrenal glands, located above the kidneys, to release stress hormones, including adrenaline (epinephrine) and cortisol.

Adrenaline, often referred to as the "emergency hormone," rapidly increases heart rate, dilates airways, and redirects blood flow to muscles, enhancing physical strength and agility. These physiological changes prepare the body for immediate action, whether it be confronting a threat head-on (fight) or fleeing from it (flight).

Cortisol, known as the "stress hormone," plays a crucial role in mobilizing energy reserves by increasing glucose levels in the bloodstream. This provides the body with a readily available source of fuel to sustain prolonged physical exertion during stressful situations.

In addition to these hormonal responses, the "fight or flight" response also involves alterations in cognitive and emotional processing. The prefrontal cortex, responsible for higher-order cognitive functions such as decision-making and impulse control, may become temporarily inhibited, while brain regions involved in emotional processing, such as the amygdala and the anterior cingulate cortex, become hyperactive.

Overall, the "fight or flight" response represents a coordinated physiological and psychological reaction to perceived threats, aimed at maximizing our chances of survival in challenging situations. While evolutionarily advantageous, chronic activation of the stress response can have detrimental effects on health and well-being, highlighting the importance of effective stress management strategies in modern life.

Environmental and Lifestyle Factors:

While neurobiological mechanisms play a significant role, various environmental and lifestyle factors can contribute to or exacerbate panic attacks:

- Stress: Chronic stress dysregulates the stress response system, increasing panic vulnerability. Effective stress management is crucial.
- Substance Use: Caffeine, alcohol, and recreational drugs can trigger or worsen panic attacks by disrupting neurotransmitter balance.
- Sleep Deprivation: Lack of sleep heightens anxiety and impairs coping abilities. Good sleep hygiene is important.
- Unhealthy Coping: Avoidance or suppression exacerbates panic long-term. Healthy coping skills like therapy are beneficial.
- Environmental Triggers: Crowded places, enclosed spaces, or trauma reminders can provoke attacks. Exposure therapy can help.

Addressing these factors holistically alongside neurobiological interventions is key for comprehensive panic management.

Practical Coping Strategies:

In addition to understanding panic's science, practical coping tools are essential:

- Deep Breathing: During attacks, deep belly breathing restores control and calms the stress response.
- Progressive Muscle Relaxation: Systematically tensing and relaxing muscles relieves physical tension.
- Cognitive Restructuring: Challenge catastrophic thoughts with realistic perspectives.
- Mindfulness/Grounding: Focus on the present moment and engage the senses to stay anchored.

Incorporating these evidence-based techniques can provide panic relief and prevention.

Personal Narrative: Sara's Experience

Sara, 28, has struggled with panic attacks for years, often in crowded or confined spaces. "It feels like my world is crumbling, even though logically I know everything is fine," she shares. "My heart races, palms sweat, and I can't catch my breath. It's terrifying."

After learning the neurobiology, Sara realized her panic was a physiological response, not a personal failing. "Understanding the science helped me realize I can manage this."

Now she uses 4-7-8 breathing, mindfulness, and healthy coping tools. "When panic starts, I take slow breaths- use the 478 technique and ground myself in the present. It's not instant, but it helps regain control."

Panic attacks can strike without warning, leaving individuals feeling helpless and out of control. Yet, there is a scientific explanation for this chaotic experience. By understanding the physiological mechanisms at play, we can gain insight into why panic attacks occur and how they impact both the body and mind. By unraveling the science behind panic, we empower ourselves to better cope with and ultimately overcome this challenge.

Chapter 3: Embracing Your Anxiety

Shifting Perspectives: Acceptance over Suppression

Anxiety is a natural and universal response to stress and perceived threats. Attempting to suppress or ignore anxiety can often intensify these feelings and lead to additional stress. Instead, acceptance involves recognizing anxiety as a normal part of life and learning to manage it effectively. This approach can improve emotional well-being and resilience.

Understanding the Physiology

When you experience anxiety, the brain's amygdala triggers the hypothalamus to activate the sympathetic nervous system. This response results in the release of stress hormones such as adrenaline and cortisol, which prepare the body for a 'fight or flight' response. These hormones increase heart rate, elevate blood pressure, and enhance alertness, which can be useful in real danger but overwhelming in everyday situations.

Strategies for Acceptance

Solution-Focused Narrative Therapy Techniques

- <u>Setting Goals:</u> Identify small, achievable goals related to managing anxiety. Instead of focusing on eliminating anxiety, focus on specific, positive changes. For instance, aim to practice a relaxation technique daily or reduce the frequency of panic attacks.
- <u>Identifying Strengths and Resources:</u> Reflect on past experiences where you successfully managed anxiety or stress. What strategies did you use? What strengths helped you cope? Highlighting these successes can empower you to apply similar strategies in the present.
- <u>Miracle Question:</u> Ask yourself, "If I woke up tomorrow and my anxiety was gone, what would be different?" This question helps visualize a preferred future and identify practical steps to move toward that future.
- <u>Externalizing the Problem:</u> Separate your identity from your anxiety by

referring to it as an external entity. For example, instead of saying "I am anxious," say "Anxiety is affecting me today." This helps to reduce self-blame and opens up space to address anxiety as a manageable issue.

- Re-authoring Your Story: Identify and rewrite the narrative around your anxiety. Focus on times when you were able to control or lessen your anxiety. Create a story that highlights your resilience and capability. This requires some journaling.
- Mapping the Influence of Anxiety: Chart how anxiety impacts different areas of your life. This can help you understand the extent of its influence and identify specific areas where you can intervene and create change.

Mapping the Influence of Anxiety Breakdown

Mapping the influence of anxiety involves examining and charting how anxiety affects various aspects of your life. This process helps you understand the extent of its impact and identify specific areas where you can intervene and create positive change. Here's a step-by-step guide to execute this technique effectively:

Step-by-Step Guide

- ❖ Identify Key Areas of Your Life:

  - Personal Well-being: Physical health, mental health, self-esteem.
  - Relationships: Family, friends, romantic partners.
  - Work/School: Performance, satisfaction, relationships with colleagues or classmates.
  - Daily Activities: Hobbies, leisure activities, daily routines.
  - Future Aspirations: Goals, dreams, ambitions.

- ❖ Create a Visual Map:

  - Use a large sheet of paper or a digital tool to create a map.
  - Place yourself at the center and draw branches extending to each key area of your life.

- ❖ Detail the Impact of Anxiety:

- On each branch, write down specific ways anxiety affects that area.
- Be as detailed as possible. For example, under "Personal Well-being," you might write "difficulty sleeping," "constant fatigue," "feelings of worthlessness."
- For "Work/School," you might note "trouble concentrating," "fear of failure," "avoiding certain tasks."

❖ Analyze Patterns and Connections:

- Look for patterns or connections between different areas. For instance, how does anxiety in your personal life impact your performance at work or your relationships?
- Identify any recurring themes or triggers that appear across multiple areas.

❖ Identify Strengths and Resources:

- On a separate part of the map or a new sheet, list your strengths and resources in each area. These might include skills, supportive relationships, past successes, or coping mechanisms.

- Reflect on times when anxiety was less impactful. What resources or strengths did you use during those times?

❖ Set Specific Goals:

- Based on your analysis, set specific, actionable goals to address the impact of anxiety in each area.
- Ensure your goals are SMART (Specific, Measurable, Achievable, Relevant, Time-bound). For example, "Practice deep breathing exercises for 5 minutes each morning" or "Schedule a weekly phone call with a supportive friend."

❖ Develop an Action Plan:

- Create a step-by-step action plan to achieve each goal. Break down larger goals into smaller, manageable tasks.
- Include timelines and checkpoints to monitor your progress.
- Monitor and Reflect:
- Regularly review your map and goals. Reflect on what's working and what needs adjustment.
- Use a journal to track your progress, challenges, and any changes in how

anxiety affects different areas of your life.

- ❖ Seek Feedback and Support:

  - Share your map and action plan with a trusted friend, family member, or therapist. Their feedback can provide new insights and encouragement.
  - Consider joining a support group where you can share experiences and strategies with others facing similar challenges.

Example

- ❖ Personal Well-being

  - Impact: Difficulty sleeping, constant fatigue, feelings of worthlessness.
  - Strengths/Resources: Good at following routines, supportive therapist, interest in mindfulness.

- ❖ Relationships

  - Impact: Avoiding social events, irritability with loved ones, difficulty expressing feelings.

- Strengths/Resources: Strong bond with a best friend, good communication skills when calm, past positive social experiences.

❖ Work/School

- Impact: Trouble concentrating, fear of failure, avoiding certain tasks.
- Strengths/Resources: Strong organizational skills, past academic/work achievements, understanding supervisor.

❖ Daily Activities

- Impact: Loss of interest in hobbies, avoiding new activities, spending excessive time worrying.
- Strengths/Resources: Passion for painting, access to a local sports club, ability to set goals.

❖ Future Aspirations

- Impact: Fear of pursuing dreams, procrastination, lack of motivation.

- Strengths/Resources: Clear career goals, previous success in setting and achieving goals, mentor support.

❖ Goals and Action Plan

➢ Personal Well-being Goal: Improve sleep quality.

➢ Action Plan:

  - Establish a bedtime routine with relaxation techniques (week 1).
  - Limit screen time an hour before bed (week 2).
  - Track sleep patterns and adjust as needed (ongoing).

➢ Relationships Goal: Enhance social interactions.

➢ Action Plan:

  - Schedule a weekly coffee with a friend (week 1).
  - Practice expressing feelings in a journal before discussing with loved ones (week 2).
  - Attend a monthly social event (week 4).

➢ Work/School Goal: Improve concentration and productivity.

➢ Action Plan:

▪ Use a planner to break tasks into smaller steps (week 1).
▪ Set specific times for focused work sessions with breaks (week 2).
▪ Seek feedback from a supervisor or mentor regularly (ongoing).

By mapping the influence of anxiety in a structured and detailed manner, you can better understand its impact and develop effective strategies to manage and reduce its effects on your life.

Make notes below on how you might begin this process, the potential value it could bring to you if utilized, and your best hopes for using this tool:

_____
_____
_____
_____
_____
_____
_____

Further Strategies for Acceptance:

Mindfulness and Awareness

<u>Mindfulness Meditation:</u> Practice sitting quietly and focusing on your breath. When anxious thoughts arise, acknowledge them without judgment and gently bring your focus back to your breath. This can reduce the intensity of anxiety symptoms over time.

<u>Breathing Exercises:</u> Techniques like 4-7-8 breathing (inhale for 4 seconds, hold for 7 seconds, exhale for 8 seconds) can help calm the nervous system. Practice these exercises regularly to enhance their effectiveness.

Cognitive Behavioral Techniques

<u>Cognitive Restructuring:</u> Identify irrational or unhelpful thoughts that trigger anxiety. Ask yourself questions to challenge these thoughts, such as "Is this thought based on facts or assumptions?" and "What evidence do I have for and against this thought?"

<u>Exposure Therapy:</u> Create a hierarchy of anxiety-provoking situations and gradually expose yourself to these situations starting from the least to the most anxiety-inducing. This controlled exposure helps diminish fear responses over time.

Lifestyle Modifications

Regular Exercise: Engage in physical activities like walking, running, yoga, or swimming. Exercise increases the production of endorphins, which are natural mood lifters, and can help decrease anxiety.

Healthy Diet: Eat a balanced diet that includes omega-3 fatty acids, whole grains, and lean proteins. Avoid excessive caffeine and sugar, which can exacerbate anxiety symptoms.

Adequate Sleep: Aim for 7-9 hours of quality sleep per night. Establish a regular sleep routine and create a restful environment to improve sleep quality.

Implementing Acceptance

Journaling: Keep a journal to track your anxiety levels, identify triggers, and reflect on your responses. Writing about your feelings can help you process emotions and gain insights into your anxiety patterns.

Support Systems: Talk to friends, family, or a support group about your experiences with anxiety. Sharing your feelings with others who understand can provide comfort and reduce feelings of isolation.

Professional Help: Consider seeking support from a mental health professional, such as a psychologist or counselor, who can offer evidence-based treatments like cognitive-behavioral therapy (CBT) or medication if necessary.

Daily Practices for Embracing Anxiety

Set Realistic Goals: Break down tasks into smaller, manageable steps. Celebrate small achievements to build confidence and reduce feelings of being overwhelmed.

Positive Self-Talk: Replace self-critical thoughts with positive affirmations. Remind yourself of your strengths and past successes to build resilience.

Relaxation Techniques: Incorporate relaxation techniques such as progressive muscle relaxation or guided imagery into your daily routine to help manage stress.

By embracing rather than suppressing anxiety, you can learn to manage it more effectively and reduce its impact on your daily life. Acceptance allows you to face anxiety with a proactive approach, enhancing your overall emotional health and resilience.

The Power of Vulnerability:

Stories of Strength Through Vulnerability

1. Navigating Panic Attacks

Consider the story of Alex, who struggled with frequent panic attacks triggered by social situations. Despite feeling ashamed and isolated, Alex decided to confide in a trusted friend about his experiences. To his surprise, the friend shared similar struggles with anxiety, fostering a sense of understanding and support. With this newfound connection, Alex felt less alone in his journey and gained valuable coping strategies to manage panic attacks. Alex's story demonstrates how vulnerability can break down barriers and facilitate mutual support in navigating anxiety-related challenges.

2. Addressing Perfectionism and Fear of Failure

Jessica grappled with crippling perfectionism and an intense fear of failure, which exacerbated her anxiety in academic and professional settings. She often struggled in silence, afraid to admit her insecurities to others. However, during a therapy session, Jessica bravely shared her struggles with her therapist, acknowledging her fear of judgment and inadequacy. Through compassionate guidance, Jessica learned to reframe her relationship with failure and perfectionism, embracing vulnerability as a catalyst for growth rather than a source of shame. By confronting her anxieties head-on and seeking support, Jessica discovered newfound resilience and confidence in navigating life's challenges.

3. Overcoming Social Anxiety

Michael's social anxiety made it challenging for him to engage in everyday interactions, leading to feelings of loneliness and isolation. However, inspired by a support group's testimonials, Michael decided to share his experiences with a close friend. Despite initial apprehension, his friend responded with empathy and encouragement, offering a listening ear and practical strategies for managing social anxiety. With his friend's support, Michael gradually exposed himself to social situations, confronting his fears and expanding his comfort zone. Through vulnerability and connection, Michael found the strength to overcome social anxiety and build meaningful relationships.

How to Embrace Vulnerability in Managing Anxiety

- Start with Self-Compassion: Acknowledge that anxiety is a common experience and treat yourself with kindness and understanding.
- Reach Out for Support: Share your struggles with trusted friends, family members, or mental health professionals who can offer empathy and practical assistance.
- Practice Exposure: Gradually expose yourself to anxiety-provoking situations in a supportive environment to build resilience and confidence.
- Reflect and Learn: Take time to reflect on your experiences of vulnerability, noting any positive outcomes or lessons learned. Use these reflections to guide future coping strategies and self-care practices.

By embracing vulnerability and sharing stories of strength and resilience in the face of anxiety, individuals can cultivate connections, receive support, and develop effective coping strategies. Through openness and authenticity, the journey of managing anxiety becomes less daunting, empowering individuals to navigate life's challenges with courage and resilience.

Chapter 4: Mindfulness and Grounding Techniques

Mindfulness Practices:

Mindfulness requires the intentional focus on the present moment, characterized by openness, curiosity, and acceptance. It involves attentively observing thoughts, emotions, bodily sensations, and the surrounding environment without applying judgment.

What is Mindfulness?

Mindfulness is the practice of paying attention to the present moment with openness, curiosity, and acceptance. It involves observing thoughts, feelings, bodily sensations, and the surrounding environment without judgment.

Key Components:

- Present Moment Awareness: Directing attention to current experiences rather than dwelling on the past or worrying about the future.
- Non-Judgmental Observation: Cultivating an attitude of acceptance and curiosity towards one's experiences, regardless of

whether they are perceived as positive or
negative.
- Purposeful Attention: Choosing where to
  focus attention deliberately, often using
  anchors such as the breath, bodily
  sensations, or external stimuli.

Benefits of Mindfulness Practices:

- Stress Reduction: Mindfulness practices
  have been shown to decrease stress levels
  by promoting relaxation and reducing
  reactivity to stressors.
- Improved Emotional Regulation: Regular
  mindfulness practice can enhance
  emotional regulation skills, allowing
  individuals to respond more effectively to
  challenging emotions.
- Enhanced Focus and Attention: By training
  the mind to focus on the present moment,
  mindfulness practices can improve
  concentration and cognitive performance.
- Greater Self-Awareness: Mindfulness
  cultivates an increased awareness of
  thoughts, emotions, and bodily sensations,
  fostering greater self-understanding and
  insight.

- Enhanced Well-Being: Research suggests that mindfulness practices can lead to greater overall well-being, including increased feelings of happiness and satisfaction with life.

Common Mindfulness Exercises:

- Mindful Breathing: Focus on the sensation of the breath as it enters and leaves the body. Notice the rise and fall of the chest or the feeling of air passing through the nostrils.
- Body Scan: Bring attention to different parts of the body, starting from the toes and moving gradually up to the head, noticing any sensations or areas of tension.
- Mindful Walking: Pay attention to each step as you walk, noticing the sensations of movement in the feet and legs, as well as the sights and sounds around you.
- Observing Thoughts and Emotions: Notice thoughts and emotions as they arise without getting caught up in them. Imagine them as passing clouds in the sky, observing them without attachment.
- Mindful Eating: Engage all the senses while eating, noticing the colors, textures, flavors,

and smells of the food, as well as the sensations of chewing and swallowing.

- Incorporating Mindfulness Practices into Daily Life:
- Set Aside Time: Schedule regular periods for formal mindfulness practice, such as meditation sessions, to build consistency.
- Integrate Informal Practice: Find opportunities to bring mindfulness into everyday activities, such as eating, walking, or washing dishes, by paying full attention to the task at hand.
- Start Small: Begin with short periods of mindfulness practice and gradually increase duration as comfort and confidence grow.
- Be Patient and Kind to Yourself: Mindfulness is a skill that develops over time, so be patient with yourself and avoid self-criticism if your mind wanders during practice.
- Seek Guidance: Consider attending mindfulness classes, workshops, or seeking guidance from experienced practitioners or mental health professionals to deepen your practice and address any challenges that arise.

Mindfulness practices offer a range of benefits for mental health and well-being, including stress reduction, improved emotional regulation, and greater self-awareness. By incorporating mindfulness exercises into daily life, individuals can cultivate present-moment awareness, enhance resilience, and foster a deeper connection with themselves and the world around them.

Grounding Techniques: Practical Methods to Stay Present During Panic.

Grounding techniques are strategies used to help individuals stay connected to the present moment and alleviate symptoms of panic or anxiety. These techniques can provide a sense of stability and safety when experiencing overwhelming emotions or sensations. Here's a comprehensive overview:

Understanding Grounding Techniques

Grounding techniques are coping strategies that focus on redirecting attention to the present moment and the immediate environment. They aim to counteract feelings of dissociation, panic, or overwhelm by fostering a sense of stability and connection.

Key Components:

- <u>Sensory Engagement:</u> Grounding techniques often involve engaging the senses (sight, hearing, touch, taste, smell) to anchor oneself in the present moment.
- <u>Physical Presence:</u> Techniques may include physical actions or movements to promote awareness of the body and surroundings.
- <u>Cognitive Distraction:</u> Some techniques utilize cognitive distraction to shift attention away from distressing thoughts or sensations.
- <u>Self-Soothing:</u> Grounding techniques can evoke feelings of comfort, safety, and relaxation to reduce physiological arousal and emotional distress.

Benefits of Grounding Techniques

- <u>Calming Effect:</u> Grounding techniques help regulate the nervous system, reducing the intensity of physiological arousal associated with panic or anxiety.
- <u>Increased Awareness:</u> By directing attention to the present moment, grounding techniques enhance awareness of one's surroundings and bodily sensations.

- <u>Improved Coping Skills</u>: Practicing grounding techniques regularly can strengthen coping skills and resilience in managing challenging emotions or situations.
- <u>Enhanced Emotional Regulation:</u> Grounding techniques promote a sense of control and empowerment, allowing individuals to regulate their emotions more effectively.

Common Grounding Techniques

- <u>5-4-3-2-1 Technique:</u> Name five things you can see, four things you can touch, three things you can hear, two things you can smell, and one thing you can taste.
- <u>Deep Breathing:</u> Focus on slow, deep breaths, counting each inhale and exhale to promote relaxation and calmness.
- <u>Grounding Objects:</u> Carry a small object in your pocket or purse that you can touch or hold onto when feeling anxious or disconnected.
- <u>Mindful Observation:</u> Notice and describe details of your surroundings, such as colors, textures, or shapes, without judgment.

- Progressive Muscle Relaxation: Tense and release different muscle groups in the body, starting from the feet and working your way up to the head.
- Self-Talk: Repeat calming affirmations or reassuring phrases to yourself, such as "I am safe," "This will pass," or "I can handle this."
- Visual Imagery: Picture yourself in a safe and peaceful place, imagining the sights, sounds, and sensations of that environment.
- Grounding Routines: Establish grounding rituals or routines, such as a daily mindfulness practice or a soothing bedtime routine, to promote consistency and stability.

Incorporating Grounding Techniques

- Practice Regularly: Incorporate grounding techniques into your daily routine, even when you're not experiencing distress, to build familiarity and effectiveness.
- Experiment and Adapt: Explore different grounding techniques to identify which ones resonate most with you. Adapt and

modify techniques based on your preferences and needs.

- Prevention and Preparation: Use grounding techniques preventively before entering potentially triggering situations or as part of a self-care plan to manage anxiety proactively.
- Seek Support: Share grounding techniques with trusted friends, family members, or mental health professionals who can provide encouragement and accountability.

Grounding techniques are valuable tools for managing panic and anxiety by fostering present-moment awareness, promoting relaxation, and enhancing emotional regulation. By incorporating these practical strategies into your coping toolkit, you can cultivate a greater sense of stability, resilience, and well-being in navigating life's challenges.

Chapter 5: Building a Support System

Understanding the Importance of Social Connections

Emotional Support:

Validation and Empathy: Social connections provide a platform for validation and empathy, allowing individuals to express their emotions without fear of judgment. Having someone who listens attentively and understands your experiences can provide immense comfort and relief.

Reduced Feelings of Isolation: Anxiety often leads to feelings of isolation and alienation. Building a support network helps counteract these feelings by fostering a sense of belonging and connection to others who share similar experiences or struggles.

Practical Assistance:

Shared Responsibilities: A strong support system involves sharing responsibilities and tasks, particularly during challenging times. Whether it's helping with household chores, running errands, or providing transportation, practical assistance from trusted individuals can alleviate stress and lighten the burden.

Access to Resources: Your support network can serve as a valuable source of information and resources related to anxiety management and mental health services. Trusted individuals may offer recommendations for therapists, support groups, self-help resources, or coping strategies based on their own experiences.

Validation and Understanding:

Non-Judgmental Acceptance: One of the most significant benefits of a supportive social network is the opportunity for non-judgmental acceptance. Being able to share your vulnerabilities, fears, and insecurities with trusted individuals who offer unconditional support and understanding can foster emotional resilience and self-acceptance.

Normalization of Experiences: Knowing that others have experienced similar challenges or emotions can normalize your own experiences and reduce feelings of shame or inadequacy. Recognizing that anxiety is a common human experience can promote self-compassion and acceptance.

Positive Influence:

Encouragement and Motivation: Supportive individuals serve as cheerleaders and motivators, encouraging you to persevere in the face of challenges and setbacks. Their belief in your abilities and strengths can boost your confidence and self-esteem, empowering you to overcome obstacles and pursue your goals.

Modeling Healthy Coping Behaviors: Observing how others in your support network cope with stress and adversity can provide valuable insights and inspiration. Positive role models demonstrate effective coping strategies, resilience, and adaptability, which you can incorporate into your own repertoire of coping skills.

Cultivating a Supportive Network

Identify Trusted Individuals:

Assess Existing Relationships: Reflect on your current relationships and identify individuals whom you trust and feel comfortable confiding in. Consider factors such as reliability, empathy, and confidentiality when selecting potential sources of support.

Expand Your Social Circle: Actively seek out opportunities to meet new people and expand your social network. Join clubs, classes, or community groups related to your interests or hobbies to connect with like-minded individuals who share common values or experiences.

Communicate Your Needs:

Open and Honest Communication: Clearly communicate your needs, boundaries, and preferences to members of your support network. Expressing your expectations and concerns openly fosters mutual understanding and respect within relationships.

Assertiveness Skills: Develop assertiveness skills to advocate for yourself and assert your needs assertively yet respectfully. Practice expressing your thoughts, feelings, and preferences assertively in various social contexts to enhance communication and assertiveness skills.

Diversify Your Network:

Seek Diversity: Cultivate a diverse support network comprising individuals from different backgrounds, ages, and perspectives. Diversity enriches your social interactions and exposes you to a wide range of experiences, opinions, and viewpoints.

Expand Your Horizons: Step outside your comfort zone and engage with individuals who possess diverse interests, skills, and experiences. Embracing diversity broadens your perspective and fosters empathy, tolerance, and cultural competence.

Quality Over Quantity:

Nurture Meaningful Connections: Focus on building deep, meaningful relationships rather than accumulating a large number of superficial connections. Invest time and effort in nurturing relationships that are based on mutual respect, trust, and authenticity.

Prioritize Reciprocity: Seek out individuals who demonstrate a genuine interest in your well-being and reciprocate their support and kindness. Prioritizing reciprocity ensures that relationships are balanced, equitable, and mutually beneficial.

Maintaining and Nurturing Relationships

Regular Communication:

Stay Connected: Foster regular communication and interaction with members of your support network through various channels, such as phone calls, video chats, or in-person meetings. Regular contact helps maintain strong connections and prevents feelings of estrangement or disconnection.

Check-In Periodically: Make an effort to check in with friends, family members, or support group members periodically to inquire about their well-being, offer support, and maintain open lines of communication.

Express Gratitude:

Practice Gratitude: Cultivate a habit of expressing gratitude for the support, kindness, and generosity of your social connections. Verbalize your appreciation through heartfelt thank-you messages, gestures of kindness, or acts of reciprocity.

Acknowledge Contributions: Recognize and acknowledge the contributions of individuals in your support network, highlighting their positive impact on your life and well-being. Expressing gratitude reinforces bonds and fosters a culture of appreciation within relationships.

Be a Supportive Listener:

Active Listening Skills: Hone your active listening skills to provide empathetic and supportive listening to others in your social network. Practice active listening techniques, such as paraphrasing, clarifying, and summarizing, to demonstrate your understanding and validation.

Offer Empathy and Validation: Show empathy and validation towards the experiences, feelings, and concerns of others, offering a safe and non-judgmental space for them to express themselves. Avoid jumping to conclusions or offering unsolicited advice, allowing individuals to explore their thoughts and emotions freely.

Reciprocity:

Mutual Support: Be willing to offer support and assistance to members of your support network when they are in need. Demonstrate reciprocity by extending kindness, compassion, and practical help to others, fostering a culture of mutual support and collaboration.

Create a Supportive Community: Collaborate with others to create a supportive community where individuals feel valued, respected, and supported. Encourage reciprocity and collective problem-solving to address common challenges and promote well-being within the community.

Building and maintaining a support system is a process that requires intentionality, communication, and reciprocity. By understanding the importance of social connections, cultivating a supportive network, and nurturing meaningful relationships, you

Engaging in social support, acceptance, and connection triggers various physiological and neurological responses in the brain, nervous system, and body.

Here's an overview of what happens at each level:

Brain:

Release of Neurotransmitters:

Social interactions and support stimulate the release of neurotransmitters such as oxytocin, serotonin, and dopamine in the brain, playing crucial roles in regulating mood, bonding, and emotional well-being.

Oxytocin, often referred to as the "bonding hormone," plays a key role in fostering trust, empathy, and social connection. It promotes feelings of attachment and closeness between individuals.

Serotonin, known as the "feel-good" neurotransmitter, contributes to mood regulation, emotional well-being, and social behavior. Increased serotonin levels are associated with improved mood and reduced anxiety.

Dopamine, involved in the brain's reward system, reinforces pleasurable experiences and motivates social engagement. It's implicated in feelings of satisfaction, anticipation, and motivation to seek social interaction.

Reduction of Stress Response:

Social support and acceptance have been shown to dampen the body's stress response and reduce the activation of the hypothalamic-pituitary-adrenal (HPA) axis.

The release of stress hormones such as cortisol and adrenaline is attenuated in the presence of supportive relationships, leading to decreased physiological arousal and anxiety.

Nervous System:

Activation of the Autonomic Nervous System:

Social support and acceptance activate the parasympathetic nervous system (PNS), which promotes relaxation, rest, and digestion.

PNS activation counteracts the sympathetic nervous system (SNS), responsible for the "fight or flight" response, thereby reducing physiological arousal and promoting a sense of calmness and safety.

Regulation of Heart Rate and Blood Pressure:

Supportive social interactions have been linked to lower heart rate and blood pressure, indicating reduced cardiovascular reactivity to stressors.

The vagus nerve, a major component of the parasympathetic nervous system, plays a role in regulating heart rate variability and promoting relaxation during social connection.

Body:

Immune Function:

Social support and acceptance have implications for immune function, with research suggesting that positive social interactions can enhance immune response and resilience to illness.

Supportive relationships may modulate immune activity, leading to improved immune function and faster recovery from illness or injury.

Pain Perception:

Social support and acceptance can influence pain perception and tolerance levels.

Supportive interactions may mitigate the experience of pain by activating brain regions involved in pain modulation and producing endogenous pain-relieving substances.
The release of endorphins, the body's natural painkillers, may be triggered by social support, leading to analgesic effects and reduced subjective experience of pain.

Engaging in social support, acceptance, and connection elicits a complex interplay of neurological, physiological, and hormonal responses throughout the brain, nervous system, and body. These responses contribute to feelings of well-being, relaxation, and resilience, while also exerting positive effects on immune function, pain perception, and stress regulation. Prioritizing social connections and fostering supportive relationships can thus have profound implications for mental and physical health, promoting overall resilience and well-being.

Communicating Your Needs: Expressing Your Anxiety to Loved Ones.

Communicating your needs and expressing your anxiety to loved ones is a crucial aspect of managing anxiety and panic effectively. Here's why it's important and some tips for doing so:

Importance of Communicating Your Needs:

Validation and Support: When you express your anxiety to loved ones, you give them the opportunity to validate your feelings and provide much-needed support. Sharing your experiences can help them understand what you're going through and offer empathy and encouragement.

Reduced Isolation:

Anxiety can often make you feel isolated and alone in your struggles. By opening up to loved ones, you break down barriers and create opportunities for connection and solidarity. Knowing that you're not alone can be incredibly comforting and reassuring.

Practical Assistance:

Loved ones may be able to offer practical assistance or accommodations to help you manage your anxiety more effectively. Whether it's providing a listening ear, accompanying you to appointments, or helping with household tasks, their support can make a tangible difference in your day-to-day life.

Strengthened Relationships:

Honest and open communication fosters trust and intimacy in relationships. By sharing your vulnerabilities and fears with loved ones, you deepen your bond and create a foundation of mutual understanding and support.

Tips for Expressing Your Anxiety to Loved Ones:

Choose the Right Time and Place: Pick a time and place where you feel comfortable and have privacy to discuss your feelings. Avoid bringing up sensitive topics during heated arguments or when either party is stressed or distracted.

Be Honest and Authentic:

Speak from the heart and be genuine about your experiences. Avoid minimizing or exaggerating your feelings, and instead, strive for honesty and authenticity in your communication.

Use "I" Statements:

Frame your concerns and needs using "I" statements to express ownership of your feelings without placing blame on others. For example, say "I feel anxious when..." instead of "You make me anxious when..."

Provide Specific Examples:

Share specific examples or instances when you've felt anxious or experienced panic attacks. Providing context helps loved ones understand your triggers and the impact anxiety has on your daily life.

Express Your Needs Clearly:

Clearly communicate what you need from your loved ones, whether it's emotional support, practical assistance, or simply someone to listen without judgment. Be specific about how they can best support you in moments of distress.

Be Open to Feedback:

Remain open to feedback and suggestions from your loved ones, even if it's not what you want to hear. Recognize that they may have valuable insights or perspectives that can help you better understand and manage your anxiety.

Set Boundaries:

Establish clear boundaries around topics or situations that are particularly triggering or distressing for you. Let your loved ones know what you're comfortable discussing and what you'd prefer to keep private.

Express Gratitude:

Acknowledge and appreciate the support and understanding your loved ones offer. Expressing gratitude reinforces positive behaviors and strengthens your relationship with them.

Communicating your needs and expressing your anxiety to loved ones is an essential part of managing anxiety and panic effectively. By fostering open, honest, and compassionate communication, you create opportunities for validation, support, and understanding in your relationships. Remember that you don't have to navigate anxiety alone, and reaching out to loved ones for support can be a powerful step towards healing and resilience.

Chapter 6: Lifestyle Changes for Anxiety Management

Consider the transformative power of lifestyle changes for anxiety management, specifically the pivotal roles of nutrition and exercise. By adopting a holistic approach to wellness, individuals can harness the profound impact of these lifestyle factors on their mental health and overall well-being. From nourishing the body with nutrient-dense foods to engaging in regular physical activity, each aspect of lifestyle modification offers unique opportunities for alleviating anxiety symptoms and fostering resilience. Join us as we explore the science behind nutrition and exercise as essential pillars of anxiety management, empowering you to take proactive steps towards a healthier, more balanced life.

Nutrition and Exercise: The Impact of a Healthy Lifestyle

It's essential to recognize its impact on the holistic well-being of individuals. Nutrition isn't just about fueling the body; it's about nourishing the mind and spirit as well. Each bite we take provides an opportunity to support our mental health and reduce anxiety symptoms. By considering nutrition from a holistic perspective, we can address the needs of the whole person—body, mind, and spirit—

and cultivate resilience in the face of anxiety. Join us as we delve into the science behind how the foods we eat can serve as powerful allies in our journey toward greater peace and well-being.

Role of Diet in Anxiety:

Nutrition is a cornerstone of mental health, and its impact on anxiety management cannot be overstated. Research suggests that certain dietary patterns, such as the Mediterranean diet, rich in fruits, vegetables, whole grains, lean proteins, and healthy fats, are associated with lower levels of anxiety and depression.

Conversely, diets high in processed foods, refined sugars, and unhealthy fats have been linked to increased inflammation and oxidative stress, which may exacerbate anxiety symptoms. Encouraging individuals to adopt a whole foods-based diet can provide the necessary nutrients to support brain health and neurotransmitter function.

Impact of Nutrients on Anxiety:

Specific nutrients play key roles in regulating mood and reducing anxiety symptoms. For instance, omega-3 fatty acids, particularly EPA and DHA, found in fatty fish like salmon and mackerel, have anti-inflammatory properties that may help alleviate symptoms of anxiety.

B vitamins, including folate, B6, and B12, are involved in neurotransmitter synthesis and have been implicated in mood regulation. Foods rich in these vitamins, such as leafy greens, legumes, eggs, and fortified cereals, should be incorporated into the diet. Additionally, magnesium, often referred to as the "relaxation mineral," plays a role in muscle and nerve function and may help reduce symptoms of anxiety. Sources include nuts, seeds, leafy greens, and whole grains.

Dietary Recommendations:

Encouraging individuals to focus on nutrient-dense, whole foods is essential for supporting mental health and managing anxiety. Emphasize the importance of incorporating a variety of colorful fruits and vegetables, lean proteins, healthy fats, and whole grains into their meals.

Providing guidance on meal planning and preparation can help individuals make healthier choices and avoid reliance on processed and convenience foods. Encourage mindful eating practices, such as paying attention to hunger and fullness cues and savoring the sensory experience of eating.

Exercise:

Benefits of Exercise for Anxiety:

Regular physical activity is a powerful tool for reducing anxiety and improving overall well-being. Exercise stimulates the release of endorphins, neurotransmitters that act as natural mood lifters and pain relievers, promoting a sense of euphoria and relaxation.

Beyond its immediate effects on mood, exercise has long-term benefits for anxiety management. It helps regulate stress hormones like cortisol and adrenaline, reducing physiological arousal and promoting a state of calmness and balance.

Moreover, engaging in regular exercise has been shown to improve sleep quality, which is crucial for emotional regulation and resilience to stress. Adequate sleep promotes cognitive function, mood stability, and overall mental health.

Types of Exercise:

Aerobic Exercise: Activities such as brisk walking, jogging, swimming, or cycling increase heart rate and oxygen consumption, promoting cardiovascular health and stress reduction. Aim for at least 150 minutes of moderate-intensity aerobic exercise per week for optimal mental health benefits.

Strength Training: Resistance exercises, such as weightlifting or bodyweight exercises, build muscle strength and endurance while also boosting self-esteem and body image. Incorporate strength training sessions into your exercise routine two to three times per week.

Mind-Body Practices: Mindfulness-based exercises like yoga, tai chi, and qigong combine physical movement with breath awareness and meditation, promoting relaxation and stress relief. These practices enhance mind-body awareness and cultivate a sense of inner peace and resilience.

Incorporating Exercise into Daily Routine:

Encourage individuals to find enjoyable activities that they can integrate into their daily lives. Whether it's walking the dog, gardening, dancing, or playing sports, any form of physical activity counts.

Suggest incorporating exercise breaks into daily routines, such as taking short walks during work breaks, practicing yoga or stretching before bedtime, or scheduling family bike rides or hikes on weekends. Making physical activity a priority and finding opportunities to move throughout the day can significantly impact anxiety levels and overall well-being.

By prioritizing nutrition and exercise as integral components of anxiety management, individuals can take proactive steps towards improving their mental health and overall quality of life. Encourage a holistic approach to wellness that encompasses both physical and mental well-being, emphasizing the interconnectedness of lifestyle factors in promoting resilience and emotional balance. Empower individuals to make informed choices about their diet and exercise habits, providing support and guidance along their journey to better mental health.

Sleep Hygiene: The Connection Between Sleep and Anxiety

By addressing sleep disturbances and promoting healthy sleep habits, individuals can effectively manage anxiety symptoms and improve their overall well-being. Poor sleep quality and insufficient sleep duration have been consistently linked to increased anxiety levels and heightened emotional reactivity. Therefore, prioritizing sleep hygiene is crucial for individuals seeking to alleviate anxiety and enhance their resilience to stressors.

Implementing strategies to improve sleep quality and quantity can lead to significant improvements in anxiety symptoms, cognitive function, and emotional regulation, ultimately supporting a holistic approach to anxiety management.

Sleep hygiene refers to a set of practices and habits that promote healthy and restful sleep. These practices are essential for maintaining optimal sleep quality and quantity, which are crucial for overall health and well-being, including mental health and anxiety management. Here's a closer look at the connection between sleep and anxiety:

Importance of Sleep for Anxiety Management:

- Regulation of Emotions: Adequate sleep plays a vital role in regulating emotions and mood. Sleep deprivation or poor sleep quality can lead to increased irritability, mood swings, and heightened emotional reactivity, making individuals more susceptible to anxiety symptoms.

- Stress Response: Sleep and stress are intricately connected. Chronic sleep deprivation can dysregulate the body's stress response system, leading to elevated levels of stress hormones such as cortisol and adrenaline. This heightened physiological arousal can exacerbate anxiety symptoms and make it more challenging to cope with stressors.

- Cognitive Function: Sleep is essential for cognitive function, including attention, memory, and decision-making. Lack of sleep can impair cognitive abilities, making it harder to concentrate, problem-solve, and regulate emotions effectively, all of which contribute to increased anxiety levels.

- Physical Health: Poor sleep is associated with an increased risk of various physical health problems, including cardiovascular disease, obesity, and diabetes. These health conditions can contribute to anxiety and further exacerbate symptoms, creating a vicious cycle of poor sleep and heightened anxiety.

Strategies for Improving Sleep Hygiene:

- Establishing a Consistent Sleep Schedule: Going to bed and waking up at the same time every day helps regulate the body's internal clock and promote better sleep quality. Consistency reinforces the body's natural sleep-wake cycle, making it easier to fall asleep and wake up feeling refreshed.

- Creating a Relaxing Bedtime Routine: Engaging in relaxing activities before bed, such as reading, taking a warm bath, or practicing relaxation techniques like deep breathing or meditation, signals to the body that it's time to wind down and prepare for sleep.

- Optimizing Sleep Environment: Creating a sleep-conducive environment is essential for quality sleep. This includes ensuring the bedroom is dark, quiet, and cool, investing in a comfortable mattress and pillows, and minimizing disruptions such as noise and light.

- Limiting Stimulants and Electronics: Avoiding stimulants like caffeine and nicotine close to bedtime can help promote better sleep. Additionally, reducing screen time before bed and avoiding electronic devices such as smartphones, tablets, and computers can minimize exposure to blue light, which can interfere with the body's natural sleep-wake cycle.

- Managing Stress and Anxiety: Practicing stress-reduction techniques such as mindfulness, progressive muscle relaxation, or journaling can help alleviate anxiety and promote relaxation before bedtime, making it easier to fall asleep and stay asleep.

Sleep hygiene is an integral component of anxiety management, with sleep quality and quantity exerting a significant influence on emotional well-being and resilience. By prioritizing healthy sleep habits and addressing underlying sleep disturbances, individuals can enhance their ability to cope with anxiety and improve their overall quality of life. Empowering individuals to adopt effective sleep hygiene practices can lead to better mental health outcomes and greater resilience in the face of life's challenges.

Chapter 7: Creativity as a Coping Mechanism

Creativity offers individuals a unique outlet to express and process their emotions, thoughts, and experiences in a nonjudgmental manner. Through artistic endeavors such as painting, writing, or music, individuals can externalize their internal struggles, finding catharsis and relief from overwhelming anxiety. Engaging in creative activities also promotes mindfulness, redirecting attention away from anxious thoughts and into the present moment. By embracing creativity as a coping mechanism, individuals can cultivate resilience, self-awareness, and empowerment in their journey towards anxiety management and emotional well-being.

Art and Expression: Therapeutic Benefits of Creativity

Expressing Creativity for Anxiety Management:

Creativity serves as a versatile tool for coping with anxiety and panic, offering diverse avenues for self-expression, emotional processing, and relaxation. Each form of creative expression provides unique benefits and opportunities for individuals to engage with their emotions and experiences. Here's a closer look at how different creative activities can support anxiety management:

Visual Arts: Painting, drawing, sculpture, and mixed media art allow individuals to externalize their emotions, thoughts, and experiences through color, form, and texture. Creating visual artwork provides a tangible means of expression and a sense of accomplishment. For example, an individual struggling with anxiety may find solace in painting abstract landscapes as a way to channel their inner turmoil into a visual representation of their emotions.

Writing: Journaling, poetry, storytelling, and creative writing offer opportunities for introspection, self-reflection, and narrative exploration. Writing allows individuals to articulate their innermost thoughts and feelings, fostering insight and understanding. For instance, keeping a gratitude journal or writing letters to oneself can help individuals cultivate a sense of perspective and resilience in the face of anxiety.

Music: Playing an instrument, composing music, singing, or simply listening to music can evoke powerful emotions and facilitate emotional release. Music serves as a universal language of expression, offering comfort, solace, and connection. Playing the piano or guitar, for example, can provide a meditative outlet for individuals to channel their emotions and find moments of peace amid anxiety.

Dance and Movement: Engaging in dance therapy, expressive movement, or physical activity promotes embodiment and emotional release. Movement allows individuals to express themselves nonverbally, connecting mind, body, and spirit. Dance classes or yoga sessions can offer individuals a safe space to explore movement, release tension, and cultivate mindfulness in their bodies.

Crafts and DIY Projects: Knitting, pottery, woodworking, and other hands-on activities provide opportunities for creativity and craftsmanship. Crafting allows individuals to channel their energy into creating tangible objects, fostering a sense of pride and accomplishment. For example, knitting a scarf or building a birdhouse can provide individuals with a sense of purpose and mastery, distracting them from anxious thoughts and promoting relaxation.

Photography and Visual Storytelling: Capturing images through photography or creating visual narratives through collage, scrapbooking, or multimedia art allows individuals to document their experiences and perspectives visually. Photography encourages mindfulness and appreciation of the present moment. Taking nature walks with a camera in hand, for instance, can help individuals connect with the beauty of their surroundings and find moments of peace amidst anxiety.

Nature and Outdoor Activities: Connecting with nature, gardening, hiking, or engaging in outdoor activities promotes relaxation, grounding, and sensory exploration. Nature-based activities offer opportunities for reflection, inspiration, and renewal. Planting a garden or going for a hike in the woods can provide individuals with a sense of connection to something greater than themselves, offering perspective and solace in times of anxiety.

Creativity offers possibilities for individuals seeking to manage anxiety and find healing and resilience. Whether through painting, writing, music, movement, crafts, photography, or nature-based activities, the act of creating provides a space for self-expression, emotional release, and connection with others and the world around us. By exploring different forms of creative expression and finding what resonates with them personally, individuals can harness the transformative power of creativity in their journey towards greater well-being and inner peace.

Engaging in art or creative expression to cope with anxiety and panic can elicit various physiological and psychological responses in the brain, nervous system, and body. Here are some of the key mechanisms at play:

Neurotransmitter Regulation:

Dopamine Release: The act of creating art or engaging in creative expression can stimulate the release of dopamine in the brain. Dopamine is a neurotransmitter associated with pleasure, reward, and motivation. Increased dopamine levels can promote feelings of enjoyment and satisfaction, providing a sense of relief from anxiety and panic.

Serotonin Modulation: Creative activities have been shown to modulate serotonin levels in the brain. Serotonin is involved in regulating mood, emotions, and anxiety levels. Engaging in creative expression may lead to increased serotonin production, promoting feelings of calmness and well-being.

Stress Reduction:

Activation of the Parasympathetic Nervous System: Art and creativity have been linked to the activation of the parasympathetic nervous system, which is responsible for promoting relaxation and reducing stress. When individuals engage in creative activities, their heart rate and blood pressure may decrease, and muscle tension may be alleviated, leading to a state of calmness and tranquility.

Cortisol Regulation: Chronic stress and anxiety can lead to dysregulation of the hypothalamic-pituitary-adrenal (HPA) axis, resulting in elevated cortisol levels. Engaging in creative expression has been shown to lower cortisol levels, reducing the body's physiological response to stress and promoting relaxation.

Emotional Processing and Regulation:

Activation of the Limbic System: Creative expression often involves tapping into the limbic system, which is involved in processing emotions and regulating emotional responses. When individuals engage in art or creative activities, they may access deeper emotional states and gain insights into their feelings and experiences, leading to emotional processing and regulation.

Integration of Sensory and Emotional Information: Creating art or engaging in creative expression involves integrating sensory and emotional information from various sources. This integration process can help individuals make sense of their emotions, reduce emotional reactivity, and enhance emotional resilience in the face of anxiety and panic.

Cognitive Flexibility and Distraction:

Activation of Prefrontal Cortex: Creative activities require cognitive flexibility and divergent thinking, which engage the prefrontal cortex of the brain. By shifting focus away from anxious thoughts and towards the creative process, individuals can experience a sense of cognitive relief and distraction from their anxiety and panic symptoms.

Enhanced Problem-Solving Skills: Engaging in creative expression fosters problem-solving skills and adaptive coping strategies. By exploring different artistic techniques and approaches, individuals can develop a sense of mastery and agency, empowering them to address challenges and navigate stressful situations more effectively.

Art and creative expression offer a powerful means of coping with anxiety and panic by modulating neurotransmitter levels, reducing stress, facilitating emotional processing and regulation, and promoting cognitive flexibility and distraction. By engaging in creative activities, individuals can harness the inherent healing properties of art to cultivate resilience, self-awareness, and emotional well-being in their journey towards anxiety management and recovery.

Journaling Prompts: Prompts for Self-reflection.

Here are several journaling prompts designed to facilitate self-reflection and exploration of emotions related to anxiety and panic:

- Anxiety Triggers: Reflect on situations, events, or thoughts that commonly trigger feelings of anxiety or panic for you. What specific circumstances tend to provoke these emotional responses?

- Physical Sensations: Describe the physical sensations you experience when feeling anxious or panicked. Pay attention to changes in your heart rate, breathing patterns, muscle tension, and other bodily responses.

- Thought Patterns: Explore the thoughts and beliefs that accompany your experience of anxiety or panic. What recurring thoughts or cognitive distortions contribute to your feelings of unease or fear?

- Emotional Responses: Identify the primary emotions you experience during episodes of anxiety or panic. Are there specific emotions (e.g., fear, worry, sadness) that tend to predominate? How do these emotions manifest in your body?

- Coping Strategies: Reflect on the coping strategies you currently employ to manage anxiety and panic. Which strategies have been most effective for you, and which ones have been less helpful? Are there any new coping techniques you'd like to explore?

- Self-Care Practices: Consider how you prioritize self-care in your daily life. What activities or practices help you feel grounded, calm, and supported? How can you incorporate more self-care into your routine to nurture your well-being?

- Support System: Reflect on your support system and the people in your life whom you can turn to for help and guidance during difficult times. How do these individuals support you in managing anxiety and panic? How can you strengthen your support network further?

- Meaning-Making: Explore the meaning or significance you attribute to your experiences of anxiety and panic. Do these experiences hold any lessons or insights for you? How do they shape your understanding of yourself and your journey?

- Goal Setting: Set specific, achievable goals related to managing anxiety and panic. What concrete steps can you take to reduce the frequency or intensity of anxious feelings? How will you measure progress towards these goals?

- Gratitude Practice: Cultivate a sense of gratitude by reflecting on the things in your life that bring you joy, comfort, and fulfillment. What are you grateful for, even amidst the challenges of anxiety and panic? How can you cultivate an attitude of gratitude in your daily life?

These journaling prompts are intended to foster introspection, self-awareness, and personal growth as you navigate your journey towards anxiety management and emotional well-being. Feel free to adapt them to suit your individual preferences and needs and remember that journaling is a personal practice — there are no right or wrong answers.

Chapter 8: Facing Fears Gradually

Facing fears gradually, also known as systematic desensitization, is a therapeutic approach commonly used in the treatment of anxiety disorders. This method involves gradually exposing oneself to feared stimuli or situations in a controlled and systematic manner, with the goal of reducing anxiety and increasing tolerance over time. The process typically begins with identifying specific fears or triggers and ranking them based on their level of distress or intensity. Individuals then work with a therapist to develop a hierarchy of exposure, starting with the least anxiety-provoking scenarios and progressing towards more challenging ones.

Through repeated and gradual exposure to feared stimuli, individuals learn to confront their fears in a safe and supportive environment, gradually building confidence and resilience in the face of anxiety. Over time, the intensity of anxiety decreases as individuals become desensitized to the feared stimuli, allowing them to engage more fully in their daily lives without being overwhelmed by fear. Facing fears gradually is an evidence-based technique rooted in principles of cognitive-behavioral therapy (CBT) and has been shown to be effective in helping individuals overcome anxiety disorders and regain a sense of control over their lives. Its science (soft science but science).

Exposure Therapy: Introduce the concept of facing fears in a controlled way.

Exposure therapy can be used effectively in the treatment of both anxiety and panic disorders. Whether someone is experiencing generalized anxiety, specific phobias, panic disorder, or another related condition, exposure therapy can help them gradually confront and overcome their fears in a controlled manner. By systematically exposing individuals to anxiety-provoking stimuli or situations, exposure therapy aims to reduce the intensity of anxiety and increase tolerance over time. This therapeutic approach is applicable to various anxiety and panic-related conditions and can be tailored to suit the individual needs and preferences of each person undergoing treatment.

Exposure therapy is a therapeutic technique used to help individuals confront and overcome their fears in a controlled and systematic manner. This approach is based on the principle of gradual exposure to feared stimuli, with the goal of reducing anxiety and increasing tolerance over time. Exposure therapy is commonly used in the treatment of anxiety disorders, phobias, post-traumatic stress disorder (PTSD), and other related conditions.

The process of exposure therapy involves creating a hierarchy of feared situations or stimuli, ranked from least to most anxiety-provoking. Individuals work with a therapist to gradually expose themselves to these feared stimuli, starting with the least anxiety-inducing scenarios and progressing to more challenging ones. Exposure can take various forms, including imaginal exposure (mentally imagining feared situations), in vivo exposure (directly confronting feared situations in real life), or virtual reality exposure (simulated exposure in a controlled environment).

Through repeated and controlled exposure to feared stimuli, individuals learn to confront their fears in a safe and supportive environment. Over time, the intensity of anxiety decreases as individuals become desensitized to the feared stimuli. This process allows individuals to develop coping skills, challenge maladaptive beliefs, and build confidence in their ability to manage anxiety-provoking situations.

Exposure therapy is grounded in principles of learning theory and cognitive-behavioral therapy (CBT). It is considered one of the most effective interventions for anxiety disorders and is supported by a substantial body of research evidence. By systematically confronting fears in a controlled way, individuals can experience significant reductions in anxiety symptoms and improve their overall quality of life.

In practical application, exposure therapy for anxiety and panic disorders involves several key steps:

- Assessment and Treatment Planning: The therapist begins by conducting a thorough assessment to understand the individual's specific anxiety symptoms, triggers, and goals for treatment. Based on this assessment, a treatment plan is developed, outlining the target fears or situations to be addressed through exposure therapy.

- Creating a Fear Hierarchy: Together with the therapist, the individual creates a fear hierarchy, which is a list of anxiety-provoking situations or stimuli ranked from least to most distressing. These may include situations related to specific phobias, social anxiety, or panic triggers.

- Exposure Exercises: The individual gradually exposes themselves to the feared situations or stimuli in a controlled and systematic manner. Exposure exercises may involve in vivo exposure (real-life exposure to feared situations), imaginal exposure (imagining feared scenarios), or interoceptive exposure (experiencing bodily sensations associated with panic). For example, someone with a fear of flying might start by looking at pictures of airplanes, then progress to visiting an airport, and eventually take a short flight.

- Managing Anxiety: Throughout the exposure exercises, the individual learns coping skills to manage anxiety and discomfort. These may include relaxation techniques, deep breathing exercises, and cognitive restructuring to challenge negative thoughts and beliefs.

- Repetition and Gradual Progression: Exposure exercises are repeated regularly, with the individual gradually facing increasingly challenging situations as they become more comfortable and confident. The pace of progression is tailored to the individual's tolerance and progress.

- Generalization and Maintenance: As the individual becomes desensitized to their fears through exposure therapy, they begin to generalize their newfound skills to other areas of their life. They learn to apply coping strategies in real-world situations and maintain their progress over time.

- Follow-Up and Adjustment: The therapist provides ongoing support and guidance throughout the treatment process, monitoring progress and making adjustments to the treatment plan as needed. Follow-up sessions may focus on addressing any remaining fears or challenges and reinforcing coping skills.

Exposure therapy for anxiety and panic disorders is a structured and evidence-based approach that empowers individuals to confront their fears in a gradual and systematic way, leading to significant reductions in anxiety symptoms and improved quality of life.

Using solution-focused narrative therapy (SFNT) techniques for anxiety, particularly in the context of exposure therapy, can involve incorporating daily practices and exercises that promote resilience, self-awareness, and progress towards anxiety management goals.

Daily Reflections: Encourage clients to engage in daily reflections where they identify moments of strength, resilience, or success in managing anxiety. They can keep a journal or use a reflective app to record these moments and reflect on what contributed to their ability to cope effectively.

Setting Daily Goals: Help clients set small, achievable goals for each day that align with their exposure therapy targets. These goals can involve specific actions or behaviors that expose them to feared stimuli in a controlled way, gradually building tolerance and confidence.

Noticing Exceptions: Prompt clients to notice exceptions to their anxiety throughout the day. When they experience moments of calm, relaxation, or mastery over anxiety-provoking situations, encourage them to acknowledge and celebrate these exceptions as signs of progress.

Strength Spotting: Practice "strength spotting" exercises, where clients actively look for evidence of their strengths, coping skills, and resilience in their daily lives. This can involve identifying times when they successfully use coping strategies, seek support from others, or challenge anxious thoughts.

Visualization Exercises: Guide clients through visualization exercises that help them imagine themselves successfully navigating anxiety-provoking situations. Using SFNT techniques such as the miracle question, ask clients to envision a day where anxiety no longer dominates their thoughts and behaviors, and explore what steps they can take to move towards that vision.

Gratitude Practice: Incorporate gratitude practices into clients' daily routines, where they intentionally focus on things they are grateful for. By shifting their focus away from anxiety and towards positive aspects of their lives, clients can cultivate a sense of perspective and resilience.

Self-Compassion Exercises: Encourage clients to practice self-compassion exercises, where they offer themselves kindness, understanding, and support when facing anxiety. SFNT emphasizes the importance of self-compassion in fostering resilience and self-esteem, particularly during challenging times.

Reviewing Progress: At the end of each day, prompt clients to review their progress towards their anxiety management goals. Encourage them to reflect on the successes they've had, the challenges they've faced, and the lessons they've learned. This daily review can help clients stay focused and motivated on their journey towards anxiety management.

By integrating these SFNT-informed practices into their daily routines, clients can cultivate a mindset of resilience, resourcefulness, and progress in managing anxiety through exposure therapy. These daily exercises serve to reinforce therapeutic principles, promote self-awareness, and empower clients to take active steps towards their anxiety management goals.

Chapter 9: Humor and Laughter in Healing

Humor and laughter play a significant role in promoting healing and managing anxiety. Incorporating humor into therapy and daily life can have several beneficial effects on mental health and well-being:

- Stress Reduction: Laughter triggers the release of endorphins, the body's natural feel-good chemicals, which can help alleviate stress and promote relaxation. Engaging in humor can provide a temporary escape from anxious thoughts and worries, offering a much-needed reprieve from tension and anxiety.

- Physical and Emotional Benefits: Laughter has been shown to have various physical and emotional benefits, including reducing muscle tension, improving immune function, and enhancing mood. By promoting a sense of lightness and joy, humor can counteract the physical and emotional symptoms of anxiety, helping individuals feel more balanced and resilient.

- Perspective Shift: Humor has the power to shift perspective and reframe challenging situations in a more positive light. By finding humor in difficult circumstances, individuals can gain a new perspective on their struggles, fostering resilience and adaptability in the face of adversity.

- Social Connection: Sharing laughter with others fosters social connection and strengthens relationships, which are important buffers against anxiety and stress. Humor can serve as a social lubricant, breaking down barriers and fostering a sense of camaraderie and belonging.

- Coping Mechanism: Humor can serve as a valuable coping mechanism for managing anxiety. By finding humor in everyday situations, individuals can build a repertoire of coping strategies that help them navigate life's challenges with greater ease and grace.

- Mindfulness and Presence: Laughter often arises in moments of spontaneity and presence, drawing individuals into the present moment and helping them let go of rumination and worry. Incorporating humor into mindfulness practices can enhance their effectiveness in reducing anxiety and promoting emotional well-being.

- Enhanced Creativity and Problem-Solving: Humor stimulates creativity and lateral thinking, which can be helpful for problem-solving and finding innovative solutions to anxiety-related challenges. By approaching problems with a light-hearted and playful attitude, individuals can overcome mental blocks and generate new ideas more effectively.

Incorporating humor into therapy sessions, daily routines, and interpersonal interactions can be a powerful tool for managing anxiety and promoting emotional well-being. Whether through sharing jokes with friends, watching funny movies, or engaging in playful activities, finding moments of humor and laughter can provide much-needed relief from anxiety and contribute to overall healing and resilience.

Humor Science:

The science behind humor and laughter involves complex interactions within the brain, nervous system, and body, resulting in a cascade of physiological and psychological effects:

Brain Chemistry: When we experience humor and laughter, various regions of the brain are activated, including the prefrontal cortex, limbic system, and brainstem. These areas are involved in processing emotions, reward, and social interactions. Laughter triggers the release of neurotransmitters such as endorphins, dopamine, and serotonin, which are associated with pleasure, mood regulation, and stress reduction. Endorphins, in particular, act as natural painkillers and promote feelings of well-being and relaxation.

Stress Response: Laughter has been shown to modulate the body's stress response by reducing the production of stress hormones such as cortisol and adrenaline. It activates the parasympathetic nervous system, promoting relaxation and counteracting the effects of the sympathetic nervous system, which is responsible for the body's fight-or-flight response to stress.

Muscle Relaxation: Laughing involves the contraction and relaxation of various muscles in the face, chest, and abdomen. This rhythmic movement promotes muscle relaxation and helps release tension, particularly in areas where stress and anxiety are commonly held, such as the shoulders and neck.

Immune Function: Studies have suggested that laughter may have immune-boosting effects, stimulating the production of immune cells and antibodies that help protect the body against infections and illness. By reducing stress and promoting relaxation, laughter may enhance immune function and contribute to overall health and well-being.

Cardiovascular Health: Laughter has been associated with improvements in cardiovascular health, including increased blood flow, improved vascular function, and reduced blood pressure. These cardiovascular benefits may be attributed to the release of endorphins, which have vasodilatory effects and promote circulation, as well as the relaxation of blood vessels during laughter.

Pain Perception: Humor and laughter have been shown to modulate pain perception and tolerance. The release of endorphins during laughter acts as a natural analgesic, reducing the perception of pain and increasing pain tolerance. This can be particularly beneficial for individuals experiencing chronic pain or discomfort related to anxiety.

Cognitive Effects: Humor and laughter stimulate cognitive processes such as creativity, problem-solving, and social cognition. They encourage flexible thinking, perspective-taking, and adaptive responses to stressful situations, which can help individuals cope more effectively with anxiety and other emotional challenges.

The science behind humor and laughter underscores their profound effects on the brain, nervous system, and body, highlighting their potential as powerful tools for managing anxiety, promoting relaxation, and enhancing overall well-being.

Laughter Therapy: Explore the role of humor in managing anxiety.

Let's break down the science of laughter therapy and its practical applications for managing anxiety:

Understanding the Science: Laughter therapy harnesses the physiological and psychological benefits of humor and laughter to promote relaxation, reduce stress, and alleviate anxiety. When we laugh, our brain releases feel-good neurotransmitters such as endorphins, dopamine, and serotonin, which contribute to mood enhancement and stress reduction. Additionally, laughter stimulates the parasympathetic nervous system, leading to muscle relaxation, improved blood flow, and reduced levels of stress hormones like cortisol.

Daily Practices and Applications:
Incorporating laughter therapy into daily life can involve various practices and activities, such as:

Watching Comedy: Setting aside time each day to watch funny movies, TV shows, or stand-up comedy specials can provide opportunities for laughter and relaxation.

Sharing Jokes: Sharing jokes or humorous anecdotes with friends, family, or colleagues can foster social connection and laughter, enhancing mood and reducing anxiety.

Laughter Yoga: Participating in laughter yoga classes or exercises, which combine simulated laughter with yogic breathing techniques, can promote deep breathing, muscle relaxation, and stress relief.

Laughter Meditation: Practicing laughter meditation involves intentionally laughing without relying on external stimuli. This mindfulness-based approach can promote present-moment awareness, emotional regulation, and a sense of inner peace.

Key Concepts to Understand: To effectively utilize laughter therapy for managing anxiety, it's essential to understand several key concepts:

Neurobiology of Laughter: Familiarize yourself with the neurobiological mechanisms underlying laughter and its effects on the brain, nervous system, and body.

Stress Reduction Techniques: Learn stress reduction techniques that incorporate humor and laughter, such as progressive muscle relaxation, guided imagery, and cognitive restructuring.

Mind-Body Connection: Recognize the interconnectedness of the mind and body in managing anxiety, and how laughter therapy can promote holistic well-being by addressing both psychological and physiological aspects of stress.

Why It Matters: Laughter therapy matters because it offers a natural, accessible, and enjoyable way to manage anxiety and improve overall quality of life. By incorporating humor and laughter into daily routines, individuals can experience immediate and tangible benefits for their mental and physical health, including reduced anxiety symptoms, enhanced mood, and increased resilience to stressors.

Value and Benefits: The value of laughter therapy lies in its ability to provide an effective, low-cost, and side-effect-free approach to anxiety management. Unlike pharmacological interventions, laughter therapy offers a holistic and empowering strategy that individuals can easily incorporate into their daily lives to promote relaxation, foster social connection, and cultivate a positive outlook on life.

Laughter therapy offers a scientifically grounded and practical approach to managing anxiety that leverages the inherent healing power of humor and laughter. By understanding the underlying science, adopting daily laughter practices, and embracing its value in promoting well-being, individuals can effectively harness the therapeutic benefits of laughter to reduce anxiety and lead more fulfilling lives.

Light-hearted Exercises: Activities to Bring Joy

<u>Funny Video Breaks:</u> Encourage readers to take short breaks throughout the day to watch funny videos or memes online. Platforms like YouTube, TikTok, or social media sites often have an abundance of humorous content that can elicit laughter and brighten the mood.

<u>Caption Contest:</u> Invite readers to participate in a caption contest where they create humorous captions for funny photos or cartoons. This activity encourages creativity, imagination, and laughter as readers come up with witty and amusing captions to share with others.

<u>Laughter Journal:</u> Encourage readers to start a laughter journal where they jot down moments of humor or joy that they experience each day. Whether it's a funny joke, a silly mishap, or a humorous observation, keeping track of these moments can serve as a reminder to find humor in everyday life.

<u>Silly Dance Party:</u> Suggest that readers organize impromptu silly dance parties at home, either by themselves or with family and friends. Put on some upbeat music, let loose, and dance like nobody's watching! Movement

and laughter go hand in hand, and dancing can be a fun and energizing way to lift the spirits.

Pun Challenge: Challenge readers to come up with puns or wordplay on a specific theme or topic. Puns are a lighthearted form of humor that can spark laughter and amusement. Encourage readers to share their puns with others and see who can come up with the most clever or amusing ones.

Pet Playtime: For pet owners, suggest spending quality playtime with their furry friends. Whether it's playing fetch with a dog, watching a cat chase a toy, or observing the antics of smaller pets like hamsters or guinea pigs, interacting with animals can be incredibly joyful and laughter-inducing.

Virtual Game Night: Organize a virtual game night with friends or family and play light-hearted games that encourage laughter and camaraderie. Games like charades, Pictionary, or online party games can provide hours of entertainment and laughter as players engage in friendly competition and silliness.

Random Acts of Kindness: Encourage readers to perform random acts of kindness for others, whether it's leaving a funny note for a coworker, sending a humorous card to a friend, or sharing a funny meme with a loved one. Acts of kindness not only bring joy to others but also cultivate a sense of connection and warmth that can elicit laughter and positivity.

These light-hearted exercises are designed to infuse joy, humor, and laughter into daily life, promoting emotional well-being and resilience in the face of anxiety and stress. By embracing moments of levity and playfulness, readers can cultivate a sense of lightness and joy that uplifts the spirit and fosters a positive outlook on life.

Chapter 10: Planning for the Future

Planning for the future is particularly valuable for individuals with anxiety as it provides a structured approach to managing uncertainty, reducing feelings of overwhelm, and fostering a sense of control. By defining a clear vision and setting specific goals, individuals can mitigate the uncertainty that often exacerbates anxiety, providing a sense of predictability and direction.

Breaking down large goals into smaller, actionable tasks makes them more approachable, reducing the risk of feeling overwhelmed and allowing for a step-by-step progression that promotes a sense of accomplishment and motivation. Monitoring progress and celebrating small victories can enhance this effect, offering tangible evidence of success and further reducing anxiety. Setting and achieving realistic goals also fosters a sense of agency and empowerment, counteracting feelings of helplessness and building confidence in one's ability to handle future uncertainties.

Additionally, sharing goals with supportive friends, family, or therapists provides valuable encouragement and accountability, reinforcing commitment and reducing isolation. Practicing self-compassion throughout the goal-setting process by recognizing that setbacks are normal and celebrating small victories can significantly improve overall mental health, reducing anxiety symptoms. This long-term approach not only helps individuals manage their anxiety more effectively but also leads to sustained personal growth and a higher quality of life.

Integrating these strategies into daily routines, such as setting daily goals, reflecting on achievements, and regularly adjusting plans, helps build a structured, supportive framework that fosters resilience and long-term well-being.

Goal Setting: Setting Realistic Goals

Planning for the future while managing anxiety involves setting realistic and achievable goals. Here's an expanded guide to help you navigate this process effectively:

Define Your Vision

Details and Clarity: Begin by creating a clear and detailed vision of what you want your future to look like. Consider different areas of your life, such as career, relationships, health, personal growth, and hobbies. Write down your vision, emphasizing specific outcomes. For instance, rather than saying "I want to be healthier," specify "I want to run a 5K within the next six months."

Positive Focus: Focus on positive outcomes. Describe how achieving these goals will improve your well-being. For example, "Running a 5K will boost my physical health, increase my confidence, and provide a sense of accomplishment."

Break Down Large Goals

Step-by-Step Approach: Large goals can be intimidating. Break them down into smaller, manageable steps. This makes the goals seem less daunting and provides a clear pathway to follow. For example, if your goal is to get a new job, break it down into steps like updating your resume, applying to jobs, and preparing for interviews.

Actionable Tasks: Each step should be an actionable task that you can complete. For instance, "Update resume" might involve tasks like "Add recent job experience," "Revise skills section," and "Proofread for errors."
Prioritize Goals

Importance and Achievability: Not all goals need to be pursued simultaneously. Prioritize your goals based on what is most important to you and what is realistically achievable in the near term. Focus on one or two goals at a time to avoid feeling overwhelmed.

Short-Term vs. Long-Term: Distinguish between short-term and long-term goals. Short-term goals should be steps that can be completed in a few weeks to a few months, while long-term goals might take years to achieve.
Set Specific and Measurable Goals

Clarity and Precision: Make sure your goals are specific and measurable. Instead of setting a vague goal like "reduce anxiety," set a specific goal such as "practice mindfulness meditation for 10 minutes each day."

Measurable Metrics: Define how you will measure success. For example, "Practice mindfulness meditation for 10 minutes each day" can be tracked by checking off each day you complete the practice.
Establish a Timeline

Realistic Deadlines: Create a realistic timeline for achieving your goals. Set deadlines for each step and adjust them as needed. This helps to maintain momentum and provides a sense of urgency without adding excessive pressure.

Milestones: Break your timeline into milestones. For example, if your goal is to

complete a certification, milestones might include "Research certification programs," "Enroll in a program by a specific date," and "Complete coursework by another date."
Be Flexible

Adaptability: Understand that goals may need to be adjusted based on changing circumstances. Be open to modifying your goals and timelines as needed. Flexibility allows you to adapt to new situations and reduces the stress of feeling locked into a rigid plan.

Resilience: Emphasize resilience. If an unexpected event disrupts your plan, assess the situation, and adjust your goals or timelines accordingly.

Seek Support

Encouragement and Accountability: Share your goals with supportive friends, family, or a therapist. They can provide encouragement, accountability, and advice. Having a support system can make the goal-setting process feel less isolating and more manageable.

Professional Guidance: Consider seeking professional guidance from a coach or therapist who can offer structured support and strategies tailored to your needs.

Practice Self-Compassion

Kindness to Self: Be kind to yourself throughout the goal setting and achievement process. Recognize that setbacks are normal and do not define your worth or ability to succeed.

Celebrate Small Wins: Celebrate small victories and learn from challenges without self-criticism. Acknowledge your progress, no matter how small, and reward yourself for your efforts.

Monitor Progress

Regular Reviews: Regularly review your goals and track your progress. Use journals, apps, or charts to keep a record of your achievements and any adjustments made along the way. Monitoring progress helps to maintain motivation and provides a sense of accomplishment.

Reflective Journaling: Keep a journal where you reflect on your progress, noting what strategies worked, what challenges you faced, and how you overcame them.
Reflect and Adjust

Ongoing Reflection: Periodically reflect on your goals and the progress you've made.

Assess whether the goals still align with your values and vision for the future. Adjust goals as needed to ensure they remain relevant and achievable.

Goal Realignment: If your priorities or circumstances change, realign your goals accordingly. This helps keep your efforts focused on what truly matters to you.

By incorporating these expanded strategies into your approach to planning for the future, you can navigate life's uncertainties with greater resilience, confidence, and self-assurance, even in the face of anxiety. Remember that managing anxiety is an ongoing process, and it's okay to seek help and support along the way.

Creating a Wellness Plan: Ongoing Self-Care

Developing a comprehensive wellness plan is essential for ongoing self-care, particularly for individuals managing anxiety. A well-structured plan promotes consistency in self-care practices and helps individuals maintain a balanced and healthy lifestyle, which is crucial for managing anxiety effectively. Here's how you can create and implement a wellness plan:

Daily Routines and Habits:

Establishing daily routines can provide a sense of stability and predictability, which is beneficial for individuals with anxiety. Incorporate habits such as regular exercise, healthy eating, and sufficient sleep. Exercise has been shown to reduce anxiety symptoms by releasing endorphins and improving mood. A balanced diet rich in nutrients supports brain health, while consistent sleep patterns enhance emotional regulation and reduce anxiety.

Mindfulness and Relaxation Techniques:

Integrate mindfulness practices such as meditation, deep breathing exercises, and progressive muscle relaxation into your daily routine. These techniques help reduce stress and promote a sense of calm. Regular practice can rewire the brain to respond more calmly to stressors, thereby reducing overall anxiety levels.

Social Connections and Support:

Cultivate strong social connections by scheduling regular interactions with friends, family, or support groups. Social support can provide emotional comfort, practical assistance, and a sense of belonging, all of which are vital for mental health. Consider joining a community group or a hobby club to expand your social network and reduce feelings of isolation.

Setting Realistic Goals:

Set achievable, realistic goals that align with your values and aspirations. Break down larger goals into smaller, manageable tasks to prevent overwhelm and promote a sense of accomplishment. Regularly review and adjust your goals as needed to stay motivated and on track.

Self-Compassion and Positive Self-Talk:

Practice self-compassion by treating yourself with kindness and understanding, especially during setbacks. Replace negative self-talk with positive affirmations and constructive thoughts. This shift in mindset can significantly impact your emotional well-being and resilience.

Professional Support:

Seek professional support from therapists, counselors, or coaches who specialize in anxiety management. Regular therapy sessions can provide you with tailored strategies and coping mechanisms to manage anxiety effectively. Don't hesitate to reach out for help when needed.

Regular Assessment and Adjustment:

Periodically assess your wellness plan to ensure it continues to meet your needs. Be flexible and willing to make adjustments based on your experiences and changing circumstances. Regular reflection on what works well and what needs improvement will help you maintain an effective self-care routine.

Practical Application for Daily Life

- Daily Routines: Begin each day with a brief exercise session, a nutritious breakfast, and a few minutes of mindfulness meditation. End the day with a relaxation technique, such as deep breathing or a warm bath, to promote restful sleep.

- Mindfulness Practices: Incorporate short mindfulness breaks throughout your day. For example, take five minutes to practice deep breathing or a quick body scan during work breaks or after meals.

- Social Interactions: Schedule weekly meet-ups with friends or family, whether in person or virtually. Participate in community events or join online support groups to stay connected.

- Goal Setting: Each week, set one or two small goals related to your personal or professional life. Track your progress in a journal and celebrate your achievements, no matter how small.

- Self-Compassion: When you encounter setbacks, remind yourself that it's okay to make mistakes. Write down positive affirmations and review them daily to reinforce a compassionate mindset.

- Professional Help: Schedule regular therapy or counseling sessions and use these opportunities to discuss your progress and any challenges you face.

By integrating these strategies into your daily life, you can create a robust wellness plan that supports ongoing self-care and effective anxiety management. This structured approach helps build resilience, promotes mental health, and enhances overall well-being, empowering you to lead a balanced and fulfilling life.

Conclusion: The Journey Continues

As you reach the end of this book, remember that your journey with anxiety management is ongoing. You've equipped yourself with valuable tools and strategies to face anxiety and panic head-on. Each step you've taken so far is a testament to your strength and resilience. The path to managing anxiety is not a straight line, and it's okay to have ups and downs. What's important is your commitment to continue moving forward.

Your progress may come in small increments, and that's perfectly fine. Celebrate each victory, no matter how small. Embrace the lessons learned from setbacks and use them as steppingstones to grow stronger. Stay connected with your support system, and don't hesitate to seek help when you need it. Remember, self-care is a journey, not a destination.

Keep revisiting the techniques that have resonated with you and remain open to exploring new strategies as you evolve. Your dedication to understanding and managing your anxiety is a powerful act of self-love. Trust in your ability to create a balanced and fulfilling life and know that every effort you make contributes to your overall well-being.

Stay hopeful, stay persistent, and most importantly, be kind to yourself. Your journey continues, and you have the strength and resources to navigate whatever lies ahead.

Recap: Summarize Key Takeaways from Each Chapter

Chapter 1: Unmasking Anxiety

Key Takeaway: Understanding anxiety involves recognizing its various forms and manifestations. Anxiety can present as physical symptoms, emotional responses, or behavioral changes. Awareness and education about anxiety are the first steps toward managing it effectively.

Chapter 2: The Science Behind Panic

Key Takeaway: Panic attacks result from a complex interplay of biological, psychological, and environmental factors. Understanding the neurobiological mechanisms, such as the fight-or-flight response, helps in demystifying panic and provides a foundation for effective management strategies.

Chapter 3: Embracing Your Anxiety

Key Takeaway: Acceptance is crucial in managing anxiety. Shifting perspectives to embrace anxiety rather than suppress it can reduce its intensity and impact. Techniques like mindfulness and self-compassion play significant roles in this process.

Chapter 4: Exposure Therapy

Key Takeaway: Facing fears gradually through systematic desensitization can significantly reduce anxiety. By creating a hierarchy of fears and exposing oneself to them in a controlled manner, individuals can build resilience and decrease their anxiety responses over time.

Chapter 5: Building a Support System

Key Takeaway: Social connections are vital for mental health. A strong support network provides emotional comfort, practical assistance, and a sense of belonging, all of which are essential in managing anxiety.

Chapter 6: Lifestyle Changes for Anxiety Management

Key Takeaway: Nutrition, exercise, and sleep are foundational elements of anxiety management. A balanced diet, regular physical activity, and good sleep hygiene support overall mental health and reduce anxiety symptoms.

Chapter 7: Creativity as a Coping Mechanism

Key Takeaway: Engaging in creative activities like art, music, or writing can serve as powerful tools for managing anxiety.

Creativity allows for expression and processing of emotions, providing therapeutic benefits.

Chapter 8: Humor and Laughter in Healing

Key Takeaway: Laughter and humor can reduce stress and anxiety by triggering positive physiological responses in the brain and body. Incorporating humor into daily life can enhance emotional resilience and improve overall well-being.

Chapter 9: Planning for the Future

Key Takeaway: Setting realistic goals and creating a structured plan for the future provides a sense of direction and control. Breaking down goals into manageable steps and celebrating progress can reduce anxiety and promote a sense of accomplishment.

Chapter 10: Creating a Wellness Plan: Ongoing Self-Care

Key Takeaway: Developing a comprehensive wellness plan that includes daily routines, mindfulness practices, social connections, and professional support is crucial for long-term anxiety management. Regularly assessing and adjusting the plan ensures it continues to meet evolving needs.

Moving Forward

Continue to apply the strategies and tools discussed in this book.

Stay committed to your wellness journey, celebrating progress and learning from setbacks.

Remember that managing anxiety is an ongoing process that requires patience, persistence, and self-compassion.

Words for Your Journey

As you journey towards understanding and managing anxiety, it's essential to recognize the strength and resilience within you. Facing anxiety head-on is no small feat, but with each step forward, you're demonstrating courage and determination.

Remember that progress is not always linear. There may be days when it feels like you're taking two steps back for every step forward. But even on those challenging days, know that you're making strides towards growth and healing. Every effort you put into understanding your anxiety and implementing coping strategies is a testament to your commitment to your well-being. You deserve that-

Be kind to yourself along the way. You are not defined by your anxiety, and it's okay to have moments of vulnerability. Allow yourself the space to experience and process your emotions without judgment. Be your own compassionate witness if you do not have one. Remember that seeking support is a sign of strength, not weakness. Whether it's reaching out to a trusted friend, a supportive therapist, or finding solace in online communities, know that you're not alone on this journey.

Celebrate your victories, no matter how small they may seem. Whether it's facing a fear, practicing a new relaxation technique, or simply getting through a difficult day, each achievement is a testament to your resilience. Take pride in your progress and acknowledge the effort you've invested in your own well-being.

Above all, keep moving forward with hope and determination. The path to managing anxiety may have its twists and turns, but with patience and perseverance, you will navigate through them. Trust in your ability to overcome challenges and embrace the journey ahead with courage and resilience.

Remember, you are stronger than you know, and brighter days are on the horizon. Keep moving forward, one step at a time, and know that you are worthy of a life filled with peace, joy, and fulfillment.

A Final Note of Encouragement:

Embrace this process with patience and self-compassion. There will be ups and downs, but each experience is an opportunity to learn and build resilience. Celebrate your progress, no matter how small it may seem. You have the inner strength and the tools to navigate through anxiety, and with each passing day, you are moving closer to a life of greater peace and control.

Believe in yourself and trust in your ability to overcome. The journey may be long, but it is filled with possibilities for growth and healing. Keep going, stay hopeful, and know that you are capable of achieving your goals. Your commitment to this journey is a powerful testament to your courage and determination.

About the Author:

K. Marlowe, PhD, is a Licensed Professional Counselor Supervisor and the founder of Next Chapter Wellness in Dallas-Fort Worth, Texas. With a strong commitment to mental health, she is a founding member of the Texas Association for Marriage and Family Therapy (TAMFT). Dr. Marlowe has dedicated her career to working extensively with trauma survivors, individuals managing obsessive-compulsive disorder, and those with dissociative disorders.

Specializing in Solution-Focused Narrative Therapy (SFNT), Dr. Marlowe approaches her work with a belief that the key to most situations lies in identifying and cultivating solutions rather than focusing on the problem. Her passion for helping others navigate through their mental health journeys is evident in her innovative and effective therapeutic approach.

Visit us at:

www.kmarlowe.com

Check out my book on mindfulness for further tools.

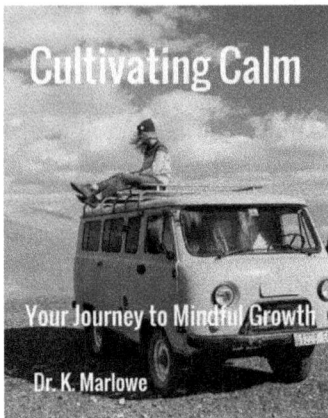

In a world inundated with relentless to-do lists, ceaseless demands, and captivating distractions, discovering the ability to be fully present within oneself has never been more essential. "Cultivating Calm" serves as your guide to cultivating a safe place within, making your mind a place of calm kindness and peaceful compassion amidst life's chaos. Explore the profound impact that being fully present has on emotional regulation, stress reduction, and the overall quality of life. From the neuroscience behind mindfulness to practical exercises for daily living, this book empowers you to design a mindscape where self-compassion thrives, purpose unfolds, and success becomes a journey of mindful growth. Embrace self-compassion, nurture connection, and embark on a purposeful exploration of the here and now.

Available on Amazon and Barnes & Noble and other retailers.

www.ingramcontent.com/pod-product-compliance
Lightning Source LLC
Chambersburg PA
CBHW070811050426
42452CB00011B/1996